Horse Training

The Comprehensive Guide To Breeding And Maintaining Rhenish German Coldblooded Horses And Saddle Up Horse Training's Comprehensive Owner's Guide To Horse Training

(Positive Reinforcement For Training A Horse To Be Harnessed)

Thanh Cardinal

TABLE OF CONTENT

Taking Care of Your Arabian Horse Essential Care for Your New Arab 1

Do you have the right mindset for training at this point? 18

Interesting Details about Your Friesian Horse 56

The Fundamentals of Horse Training or Horse Retraining 100

Tips for Beginning Equine Trainers ... 123

Taking Care of Your Arabian Horse Essential Care for Your New Arab

It is much easier to prevent future health issues with your Arab horse if you start learning to take care of him before bringing him home. For every stage of his life, it is crucial to properly feed, groom, and exercise your Arab. Before bringing him home, you should have a veterinarian checkup. Oh, and be advised that he will likely resist or show signs of dread on your first visit. He will rapidly become friendly with the veterinarian and build trust before further visits. Keeping him cognitively and physically engaged throughout his life will reduce negative behaviors.

Consuming

The nutrition of your horse is crucial to its overall health. His age, degree of exercise, and breed will all influence his dietary requirements. Make sure you choose the right meal for his health. Here are some tips for feeding your horse and suggestions for the kinds of feed to use.

Dehydrated Animal Feed

Be sure to prioritize past feedings by the previous owner when selecting dry fodder. Alfalfa is preferred over grass hay by many horse owners. Legumes like Alfalfa are higher in protein than grass hay. When Arabs consume that much protein, some of them become "jacked up." Pay carefully if your horse seems more lively or shows signs of behavioral issues. Try grass hay, like Timothy Hay or Orchard Grass, for a week if you observe this behavior and see if it stops. You should convert your horse to a grass hay diet if you discover that the Alfalfa is making them hyperbolic.

Extra Vitamins, Grain, or Feed

Pick a horse food with a wide variety of vitamins and minerals.

Supplements have been developed for all horses, including young, elderly, fat, and athletic horses. Super Supplement LMF - G is a vitamin supplement feed that I prefer to use. G is an acronym for grass hay. If you are giving your horse Alfalfa, you must get another variety. I feed ½ pound of LMF-G to my Arabian horses in the morning and evening. Additionally, they are given one pound of COB twice daily, a blend of maize, oats, and barley. Due to recent weight loss, my eldest senior horse is fed an additional ½ pound of rice bran twice a day to assist her in putting on weight.

Following their morning meal, the horses are released into the pasture during the dry seasons. For the most of the day, they can graze on the grass.

They can eat almost a pound of grass in a single hour. Ensure every horse has extra hay overnight if allowed to graze for ten hours. Most Arabian horses weigh about 1000 pounds, with the shoulder and greatest point of the body measuring 15 hands. Pasture and grass should be fed to a horse of this size daily to reach 20 pounds. Give your horse an extra 10 pounds of hay in the evening for the night on days when it's believed that he grazed 10 pounds of grass.

You may keep your horse inside the paddock on certain days due to inclement weather. You must provide each horse with about 20 pounds of hay in their stall on those days. The grass has a very high sugar content in the early spring. Most horses should only spend a brief period in the pasture in the spring when new growth is expected. In some years and locations, there is a second new growth season in the fall. Because every nation's region is unique, pay attention to where you live.

This restriction on lush, quick-growing grass is due to the possibility of your horse overindulging in sugar and developing "founder." A horse that experiences a fall may rapidly acquire laminitis. Your horse may become severely crippled or perhaps die from laminitis. Limiting pasture time at these times of fresh grass growth is a safer way to prevent disease.

Wet Cuisine

Arabian horses that are elderly and toothless may benefit from a diet high in moist horse food. If a horse cannot chew its hay, it can be replaced with soaked hay pellets. To prolong your horse's life, feed it soaking pellets even if it hasn't had teeth in years. Typically, your horse may begin to lose teeth at 25. They might not need to transition to a wet diet for at least five years.

Diet of Fresh Foods

Your Arab may benefit greatly from a fresh food diet because it more closely resembles what he would consume on his own in the wild. However, if he is fed only grass, you must be careful not to let him get fired. Many horses can survive without extra hay, food, or vitamins. Plenty of horses can live in pasture year-round without ever getting laminitis. We would advise installing an automated irrigation system.

How Much Your Arabian Horse Should Be Fed

The amount of food you provide your Arab depends on his size, age, activity level, and endurance. If you can feel your horse's ribs, you can determine if he needs extra food. You can tell if you feed him enough if his ribs are not showing through. You will need to reduce his feed if he starts to get fat on his ribs. The following is a general feeding guideline for grass or hay: Every day, 2% of the horse's body weight. This is predicated on the projected quantity of nighttime hay and/or pasture grass.

Remember that this is only a general guideline you can modify as necessary. However, remember that an adult Arabian horse weighs approximately 1000 pounds. Therefore, you should feed him about 20 pounds of hay or grass daily.

When Your Arabian Horse Should Be Fed

Arabs must eat continuously throughout the day to consume 20 pounds of hay daily. I've witnessed show horses confined to stalls for up to 23 hours daily. I've witnessed them being kept in the stall under heat lamps and blankets in the winter. They take this action to prevent the horse from developing a winter coat. In the world of show horses, a winter coat is not fashionable. If you owned a show horse, we think you would probably buy a training guidebook tailored specifically to show horses instead of this book.

The majority of people do not board horses in pastures without the need for regular feeding. Most Arabs will be fed twice daily, morning and evening. You will allow your horse to graze in the pasture for most of the day following the morning feeding. Your Arab will learn after a few days that the evening feed consists of some grain and vitamins. When you call your Arab into his paddock to give him the grain he wants, he will anticipate it. They adore grains and vitamins. It resembles a prize or a treat. They will soon pick up on the fact that you should yell his name or give a loud, sharp whistle. When you call him in, find a safe spot to stand since he might charge you at full speed. It is doubtful your Arab will run you over, but it is safer to stand near a fence post or something that you know he won't run into for your security. You will eventually gain enough confidence in your Arab to know that he won't ever touch you or run you down when entering their pasture.

Feeding your Arab twice a day provides more time for training, socialization, and bonding. Your Arab will come to identify you by providing their preferred food: vitamins and grains. You will become his favorite human and will undoubtedly go up a notch if you feed your Arab twice a day (personally). If you feed him, this dynamic will probably happen sooner.

Being the herd's alpha leader and establishing your dominance are important aspects of horse management. For the time being, being an Alpha Status means you get to eat first; we explore this in our last chapter. Although it might appear insignificant, it plays a significant role in developing your alpha. Your Arab needs to be patient when it comes time for him to eat. By doing this, you demonstrate your control and educate your Arab that you are in charge. Even before you call him in, he can wait in his paddock for feeding time. This will not happen every time the grass is in its active growing season. He may choose the sweet new grass growths over his grain during that time. To teach your Arab, you might need to walk outside with him, put a halter on him, and take him to the paddock a few times. If he has a pasture companion that enters immediately, your Arab will probably follow him the first few times.

Changing Foods

It can eventually become evident that, for various reasons, switching to hay or grain is necessary. Try this switching schedule to switch food brands:

Day 1-2: Blend ¼ new and ¾ old food items.

Combine days 2–4 with day 1

Day 5–6: Combine ½ new and ¼ old. All of the newly introduced food

As mentioned before, you should start slowly while changing your Arab, for example, from Alfalfa to Orchard Grass Hay. Because Alfalfa has a greater protein content than other grasses, you might notice that your hotblooded Arab is becoming more energetic. It would be wise to try him on Orchard Grass. You'll probably notice that his conduct has improved. You could use "Mare Magic" on your Arab mare to balance her mood based on her cycles. Her behavior will probably improve, and you will notice it. Mare Magic can likewise lift a Gelding's mood. You might cut your horse's diet after noticing he has too much fat around his ribs. To help your horse gain weight again, you can add some rice bran to his diet after seeing that you can feel or see his ribs. It is typical to alter or modify your Arab diet to preserve optimum health. You are advised to contact your veterinarian for further guidance if you are unsure.

Healthy Snacks and Treats

You can include the following nutritious human items in your Arab's diet or give him as treats:

A delight of oats and molasses

Oatmeal and apple snacks

Apples

Arable Fruits

Different treats for horses from your feed store

Pumpkin or squash

Carapace

Working Out Your Arab

For the health of your Arab, exercise is vital. Arabs require exercise to keep healthy, just like people. As an Arab age, he is more likely to experience weight, joint, muscular, and cardiac issues due to his sedentary lifestyle. You want to give your Arab lots of exercise and unstructured outdoor play in his paddock.

Arabs need to exercise for thirty minutes to two hours every day. Arabs require two hours or more of exercise and pasture time. You may give him some of this exercise by letting him run around in his pasture. You need to be proactive about some of these activities. When he has finished his feed in the morning, go into his paddock, put on his halter using the lead line, and tie him (leaving some slack) to the hitching rail.

Get out his brushes and brush his whole body completely. Remove all the tangles by brushing his mane and tail. If you brush your Arab's mane and tail daily, you will not notice many tangles on the second and third days. After brushing, put on your Arab's blanket and saddle if you plan to ride him for the day's exercise.

It's crucial to give your Arab a thorough brushing each time before mounting.

Make sure you brush out any burrs, foxtails, and dirt. You will not have a happy Arab if you saddle him with a burr between his skin and the saddle. We advise taking lessons before you ride your Arab if this is your first horse and you have never done so. Additionally, you can learn how to bridle and saddle your Arab. You can put on his harness after adjusting the cinch of his saddle. Fasten his reins to the saddle horn (in the case of a western saddle) or, in the case of an English saddle, around the base of his neck close to the saddle. If you have a round enclosure, attach his long lead rope and take him to the middle of an empty pasture.

To warm up your Arab's muscles, you can exercise him by having him walk, trot, or canter around you. We will talk more about particular exercise training later. As a general guideline, perform ten canters, ten trots, and ten circles to walk to the left. Walk, trot, and canter to the right, then reverse course and repeat. He will be warm enough to ride after this. Additionally, it will help him release some of his stored energy, improving his behavior when riding after.

You're prepared to ride now. You could employ a mounting block to minimize lifting your leg high enough for your stirrups. Still, you must be able to mount in both directions. Introduce him gently. Ride him for 10-15 minutes the first time. The following day, try 15-20, then 20–25, and so on, following the same pattern until you reach one hour a day. As long as you are riding in an indoor ring, nothing should go wrong. Your Arab can feel afraid to leave the stable if you head out to ride on a trail.

You might need to make a few shorter outings when you first leave the stables. You are less likely to run into issues if you have been riding for at least a week after bringing your Arab to the stables. A condition known as "barn sour" may cause your Arab to become more fearful if you wait more than a week. This indicates that your Arab fears venturing out of his comfortable stables and into the unknown or desert.

Do you have the right mindset for training at this point?

The trainer needs to be in a good mental state for training to be effective. The training won't go very far if he is scared or distraught. The best training occurs when the horse is curious, calm, and satisfied. When the horse emerges from this condition, the trainer must determine how to redirect and concentrate his attention. If a training object, like a whip or tick, causes the horse to feel fearful, back off and spend some time desensitizing the horse until it is more relaxed once more. If the horse is distracted by something else (maybe another horse is galloping nearby), try to find a method to get their focus back on you. You might keep your horse moving or ask for easy exercises that you are confident your horse can perform. If something you did hurt the horse, or if he is becoming bored with the training, stop and give him some attention, or simply take him for a leisurely walk until he calms down. Then, you can resume the training, beginning with more easy exercises and plenty of rewards to make the experience enjoyable. Don't waste time working with a highly stressed or excited employee. The horse won't be able to concentrate on your training, and you will undoubtedly become frustrated.

This same principle applies to you as well: stop! If you are exhausted from a long day at work or simply feel like you and your horse are losing touch. Pick up your training again on a different day, rather than pushing past your mental boundaries and possibly doing something you will later regret and set your training back.

Ten horses training for success and removing obstacles

Owners of horses are frequently plagued by rudeness and behavior from their horses that is just dangerous. People who talk about their experiences will talk about pushy horses, biting, kicking, rearing, and bucking, as well as the horse that won't go. While everyone talks about these as distinct issues, did you know they are all related to one of two causes?

The primary issue with training horses is not developing trust and establishing a leader-follower relationship. Fortunately, a systematic program guides you through this process based on how horses naturally behave and think. Hereareten horse training techniques tohelpyou get started.

1. LÑNGUG T KING BƎDΣ

Horses use their body language with great care and attention. They are mute but communicate with each other in the herd using body language. Thebodylanguageyou'reusing demonstrates whetheryou'realeaderor a follower. Being a leader doesn't have to mean being abusive. It just requires a self-assured stance and a lack of uncertainty. Maintain a straight gait and look where you're going. First, go through the gates. Breathe deeply to keep your thoughts relaxed and to lessen your anxiety. Horses recognize and utilize all these cues to determine their place in the herd.

2. D*T R*L* \N TR*T

There's an appropriate moment to give your horse a treat, such as when you're lounging in the pasture or gardening. Avoid using tactics to try to change behavior. This implies not giving treats like carrots when brushing, loading, or requiring your horse to perform any tasks. Using treatments to moldbehavior will make your horses perceive you differently.

3. LΔïD A HR'IE PR\ΠERLΣ

People don't give leading their horses much thought unless in cases when there are issues like the horses becoming pushy or dragging. That's awful since you have to size up to see who is in charge of the "herd" when leading the horse. Initially, avoid holding the lead rope next to the heater. Hold it down the line 12 to 18 inches. Hold the rope loosely; avoid pulling it tight out of an attempt to control your horse based on fear.

Additionally, hold the rope loosely in case the horse decides to bolt rather than wrapping the end around your hand. Watch your posture next. Is the horse stepping on you when you're strolling? Does he take one or two more steps when you reach a stop? If so, he views himself as the herd leader, or at the very least, he challenges you. Work on this by reestablishing your position as he passes you by by shifting directions. Take some time to stroll and explore. Step back from your horse (remember to place yourself in front of it), raise both hands and breathe.

4. TEMPHPÕRENÏL SPACE LIMITS

People frequently wonder why natural horsemanship instructors spend so much time grooming their horses. This is because establishing a boundary for personal space and respect is necessary for safe handling. Ensure the lead rope is wound from side to side to get your horse back up. Next, pay attention to personal space norms. Create a virtual bubble that the horse will never be able to enter. When he does, support him. Of course, you can enter his space to pet and treat him (when not training), but he cannot decide when to come into your life.

5. Make use of round pen training

Start with a few round-pen training sessions while starting with training or solving any kind of problem. This fundamental training tool builds trust with your audience and demonstrates leadership and respect. The instruction is "at liberty," which entails going around the pen and removing the lead rope. Move your horse in a body language manner and watch for signals of communication from them. View my article about horseback riding for more information.

6. CREATE A TRAINING GROUND ON THE GROUND FIRÅT

Another common inquiry regarding natural horsemanship is: "Why are you spending all of your time playing with the horse on the ground?" Horses are for riding, right? Of course, they're meant for riding! Teaching indications for riding on the ground first is the aim of ground training. It is safer to introduce the horse to significant injuries on the ground and aids in reinforcing the leadership skills you developed when leading and round pen training. Teach the horse his cues on the ground first and thencarry it over tothe saddle.

7. DO NOT DIE MINDLÕ˙˙ LUNGING

One of the most important training tools for horseback riding or working with an experienced horse is being prepared to ride and lunge a horse. That is the case if you don't mindlessly lunge—if you just have the horse go in circles to wear him out. How often have you heard someone declare they are about to "wear out" or "calm down a hot horse"? Plunging is ineffective; having a famous athlete train her on a track would exhaust her. It strengthens and becomes more athletic. Use lunging as a teaching tool to help the horse learn to listen to your commands to get something from it. Begin by letting the horse walk first. Work on direction changes and stopping. After that, try to get him to trot and finally go for a walk. Come cantering in when she has gotten to know you well at the trot. Plunging should be done with attention and lightness in mind. A horse will not untangle itself if you ask him to stop trotting to a walk while lunging.

8. DRƎΠ TH'Y HEAD

Dropping the head is a common communication cue leaders use to indicate acceptance of you as their leader and convey a relaxed state of mind. His head was raised, his eyes protruding, a dog on high alert for danger. A horse without fear shows his head down, so perhaps he can obtain some food! Encourage relaxation and acceptance of your leadership role by intentionally slowing down the pace of life. Hold one hand above the head and use the other to pull down on the lead rope. Hold tight until he bows his head, and then let go.

9. HEAVY RELEASED FRÞM THE RELEASE

This leads us to the next crucial aspect of horse training: horses absorb lessons from their experiences. Applying pressure is the equivalent of asking for something. On the ground, you push on a certain body part, such as the hip, to get him to move it away from you in the area where your leg is stuck. The return for the hunt is the release of the pressure. Upon your horse doing the requested task, release the pressure instantly.

10. FLX

One of the most crucial training activities is flexibility. Position yourself at the ends and utilize the lead rope to let the horse rotate his head completely without requiring him to move. This accomplishes two goals: it trains the horse for the emergency one-rein stop, making riding safer, and it makes the horse nice and light for cues you'll provide while riding.

That's all! These ten-hour training guidelines will assist you in creating a strong foundation with your horse.

3 What's Your Maximum Pace?

There are many things to consider when searching for a barrel racing potential. Which bloodlines are your favorites? Are you looking for a stud, gelding, or mare? When you begin training a horse, what age do you wish them to be, and how advanced do you want them to be?

Are you drawn to a short, stocky gelding?

Or would you rather ride a sixteen-hand mare with long legs?

When selecting a barrel racing prospect, there are many factors to consider, and some characteristics will dictate how soon you reach your objectives.

That raises another point to think about: what are your objectives?

Would you rather compete in professional rodeos or local races?

Regarding futurities, what say you?

Is riding a serene and laid-back horse that can win the 3D race in less than a second enjoyable? Alternatively, would you have the courage and expertise to take on the fastest ride of your life by riding a fire-breathing dragon down an alleyway?

I was looking for a new challenge, having lost yet another barrel horse's potential to lameness that would end his career. I started looking through page after page of internet advertisements, examining horses of various ages, pedigrees, and training levels. It was challenging to decide which would best serve my objectives. Not just my goals but also my budget. There were great prospects for $10,000 horses, but those were way out of my price range. I've never had a big spending plan. This has frequently led to me purchasing items with little to no promise to turn a profit. Next time, utilize that profit to purchase a better possibility. As a trainer, I know I can teach a horse to run barrels, but the horse's ability directly affects the level of competition and the speed at which they attain their maximum potential.

Less expensive but requiring more preparation time, a young horse (under four) is not yet ready to learn the barrels. Young horses must be well-mannered and knowledgeable about the fundamentals, including cue-based lead catching, bit yielding, proper halting, and smooth, steady body language when riding. Those abilities are essential for being ready to react when you ask them to pick up the talent of turning a barrel. Horses differ in their rates of mental and physical development. Like people, some horses reach maturity early in life, while others must reach a certain age before developing the necessary motor skills and mental toughness to begin working.

If they haven't already begun learning the barrel pattern, older horses, often between the ages of five and seven, are well-broken and prepared to learn it.

They normally cost extra because of how far advanced they are in their training.

Price is typically also influenced by bloodlines. I have witnessed a wide range of trends in the history of barrel horses during my lifetime. Nearly everyone used to compete on whatever old cow horse their dad had in the pasture when I was a little child. After that, everyone began purchasing horses off the racecourse because they needed more speed. Although those horses were fast, they frequently lacked the necessary skills for turning and had difficulty becoming steady when around three barrels. Everyone started buying cutting rejects in exchange for better turns. Horses that were adequately broken and of the appropriate age to begin training on the barrels did not become excellent cutters. Then, an immensely popular and successful professional barrel racer arrived on her five-hundred-dollar feedlot reject. Everyone wanted to try their luck with a horse derived from working cattle in feedlots once she succeeded. Because horses are now bred especially for the barrel racing sport, prices for horses of the same age and ability level might differ significantly depending on which bloodlines are in vogue.

The fastest time to go from starting the pattern to being prepared to haul to races would be a well-broken horse, not begun on barrels, that was in my price range and around four or five years old. I looked for one that appealed to me and fit my budget. After weeks of thumbing through advertising, I finally spotted an ad and figured out how far away I was ready to travel to even look at a potential horse.

"Three-year-old Gelding AQHA." Paid in full by December of the next year and got to work on the barrels... $5,000

The advertisement included a photo of a large, gorgeous bay gelding. He was being escorted by a tiny boy who looked around six years old, and he was sparkling like a new penny. The gelding moved casually, keeping his head down and trailing the young lad. With his tiny partner, he appeared to grasp that he needed to use caution. I didn't find anything particularly appealing about the bloodlines. I wasn't sure how broken this horse would be because Hancock-bred horses were notorious for bucking. He was being utilized on a North Texas ranch and was described in the advertisement as kind. The commercial featured videos of a cowboy roping and hauling a barrel through a grass-ground arena. A woman was seen loping him around the barrels in another video. Though he appeared willing to comply with her requests and had a nice gait, I could tell she was having difficulties with him on the first barrel.

To even give him a try, how far would I have to drive? That query was promptly addressed, as were a couple more I had for the owners. He had grown up with them on their ranch near Amarillo. I would have to drive eight hours to see him, which was a significant distance. If I decided I wanted him, I'd also need to take a trailer because I didn't plan on driving back.

It turned out that finding the ranch wasn't too difficult, and the drive was rather enjoyable. I could look at his sire and dam; the owners had both available.

The pair alternatedly mounted the gelding to demonstrate his abilities to me. He was as silent as he appeared in the videos. After roping him, they led him through the pattern in a lope. As indicated earlier, I could tell he was fighting the first barrel when I rode him next. I wasn't too concerned about it because I knew he wouldn't be difficult to mend. I found him appealing because he seemed quite laid back and didn't seem afraid of a rope. The fact that he was so attractive further drew me in. His thick, glossy mane and tail were both very lengthy. Though he was supposed to grow to sixteen hands, his parents were not particularly tall horses. He genuinely wanted to please whoever rode him and had a kind gaze.

Next, we started the haggling because I had asked if they would be open to negotiating the price. We quickly agreed on a cheaper cost than initially stated, so I packed him up and left for home.

The lengthy drive home was so thrilling! I did study on the futurity because he was already fully compensated for a tournament that would take place the following year. The admission costs alone had been $1,700. That was a lot more money than I had ever invested. That was how much I had paid for horses, but I had never paid that much for entrance! I had a year to train him on the barrels and then run him at the futurity as a four-year-old after purchasing him in November when he was three. I was thrilled about my new opportunity and up to the challenge!

I called him Pistol, and he was kind. He didn't buck, unlike what I understood about most Hancocks. Sometimes, when you initially ask him to lope, he could get a little hopping with his back feet if he hasn't been ridden in more than a week, but he usually rides out of it. He kept growing, standing at nearly fifteen hands tall. It was delightful to clean and style his long, thick black mane, but for competitions, it had to be constantly braided to prevent your hands from becoming tangled in it. His tail was equally lengthy and thick, trailing the earth after him.

Shortly after he settled in, training started. Timing the first barrel was challenging. To the right, he was more rigid than to the left. He would turn the first barrel without fighting the bit, but he had trouble controlling his timing. He slowed down too much and didn't sit on his back end and turn the first barrel if I pulled him too fast. He would have to flare out wide as he went off for the second barrel if I pulled too late, and he would have to shoulder into it. I devised an activity where I would push him until he stopped in the exact area. To be in a position to make a decent turn, he needed to sit down and turn at that point. It became more my job than his to make the proper movements for a flawless turn once he started to grasp time.

He had no issue navigating his second or third barrels; both left turns. Soon after, we began accelerating and following the pattern.

Young horses, in my opinion, require time to mature. I tried to be patient and not push Pistol too hard when I saw that he wasn't going as fast as he could because pushing them too hard too soon can have negative effects on both their emotional and physical health. The ability to run more quickly should come with age. I, therefore, hauled him for displays throughout the year, allowing him to pick up speed at his rate. He gained confidence in his turns by the end of the year, and I could ask him for everything without worrying that we would make mistakes.

It was rather cold when we visited the Oklahoma futurity in December. We were both freezing often, yet winters in Southeast Texas don't get very cold. Though not particularly quick, our warm-up runs were fluid. I made an effort to be calm. He consistently finished a second or a second and a half below the winning times at local contests. Although I knew I wouldn't be able to perform well in the future, I would still find it respectable and relish the experience of being part of such a big event. By the third day, he had slowed way down. He felt more lethargic than I had ever felt during our last run. I asked for all he had, whipped and kicked him, but it didn't accomplish anything. My instinct told me there was a problem. He didn't feel like himself and was two seconds off the winning times.

The fact that he hadn't even performed as well as he had a few weeks prior at local races was more concerning than the fact that the futurity didn't go well. Pistol started coughing two days after he got home. At first, I didn't give it much thought, but after more than two weeks, I realized he was ill. He developed pneumonia when I eventually took him to the vet. Although not life-threatening, it was serious enough that I would have to spend around three months away from him while he recovered and got treatment.

He continued to cough after three months. Three more months of treatment were needed because the medication was insufficient to combat the virus. I was not around for practically the whole of Pistol's fifth year. I had hoped he would continue his training; it was a great letdown.

When he turned six, I resumed working with Pistol on the barrels. As he grew stronger, we resumed our racegoing. He remained in the 3D (one second behind the winning time). I felt irritated. I had assumed he would pick up speed, but it seemed like he was reaching his limit. It didn't appear that he was passionate about running. He simply followed the motions while I kicked and whipped him every step of the way through the sequence. He was usually calm and never got excited. He was so smooth and slow at a trot and lope that he was a pleasure to warm up. Although it was enjoyable to ride, running with him wasn't pleasurable.

I felt irritated. The horse, I assumed would get faster as he aged had decided he was moving quickly enough and didn't want to move any faster. Although he had a lot of speed, his heart wasn't in it.

Next steps: what should I do?

I asked for help because I knew many people in the horse world. I felt Pistol would be better in the show ring after slowing him down even more at a trot and lope, so I asked them what they thought. They both thought he could be competitive in several sports.

Pistol was intended to be a show horse, but not the kind that competed in the AQHA world show. He could compete in ranch pleasure and trail, and there were new associations for stock horses. Additionally, he was a good fit for horsemanship in regular horse competitions. Despite my lack of experience in this subject, I tried my best to prepare him for the competition.

During his first few performances, this once-barrel futurity horse did well! Despite our lack of experience, we both placed multiple times. Every time they mentioned our names in the placements, I was utterly amazed by both of us and taken aback.

One nice woman rode up to me and asked me about my horse. She looked like she had just competed in the AQHA World Show because of her matching attire and silver accented saddle.

How did you obtain him? She uttered those words.

She had seen our placement in several events.

"Well, roughly six months ago, I was running barrels on this horse," I retorted. I thought seeing how slow he could go would be best because he wasn't barreling very quickly.

She found it unbelievable! Her expression was one of total shock!

"I just felt he was not at his best running barrels, so I gave him a chance to do something he might enjoy," I said with a smile. "I like my horses to be happy with their job."

He was turning into a fairly nice showhorse, she had to admit.

Not every potential customer turns out to be a profitable client. Sometimes, you must admit that maybe barrel racing isn't the proper career for that person. A competent trainer must recognize when a horse is not enjoying their work, and if you want them to excel at it, you must find something they enjoy doing! Even if it is not what you enjoy.

I listed Pistol for sale because I didn't want to show it, and soon, I had some interested parties. As it occurred, his original owners from North Texas contacted me. Their goal was to repurchase him. I gladly obliged, and to the best of my knowledge, he remains on the ranch with them working cows.

Interesting Details about Your Friesian Horse

Naturally loving creatures, Friesian horses seek to please their owners.

The Friesian Horse is a well-established breed that has global recognition.

Contemporary Friesian horses are invariably black.

The Netherlands is where the Friesian Draught Horses first appeared in the fourth century.

A Belgian Black was a common nickname for the Friesian Horse.

Although they are still utilized for work, Friesian horses are also used for dressage, show, and pleasure.

The Friesian Horse has been used for riding since it was first produced as a working horse.

The contemporary Friesian Horse makes a fantastic riding horse.

The Friesian Horse has demonstrated aptitude in dressage and horse competitions.

Worldwide, there are about 45,000 Friesian horses.

Section Three

Getting Your Friesian Horse Socialized

How to Train Your Friesian Horse to Be Happy Around People

It's crucial to socialize your Friesian Horse early on. Are you aware of the reason? A well-socialized Friesian horse does not react negatively toward or fear dogs or people. He is aware that both people and dogs exist and do not always threaten his safety. Unsocialized Friesian horses, on the other hand, experience dread and perceive the outside world as a threat. The presence of people or other canines frightens and threatens him. Therefore, you must begin socializing your Friesian Horse when you bring him home. Acclimate him to living with pets and other people.

Viewpoint (Yours)

Your Friesian Horse can tell a lot about your attitude. You are like a book to him. He can tell when you are angry with him. Additionally, he can detect when you are upset and won't accept that it isn't related to him. As a result, you should always be forceful and have a positive attitude while socializing. When your Friesian Horse senses your positive energy, they will bond more strongly. Be kind, loving, patient, and supportive at all times.

Express your pride and joy more than your annoyance or dissatisfaction. If you are frustrated, take a moment to yourself, take a deep breath, and engage in a different activity with your Friesian Horse. Come back when you're feeling composed and at ease. Your secret to success while teaching your Friesian Horse will be positivity. Avoid being enraged or persistently pushing your Friesian Horse, as this will negatively impact your training experiences and overall outcomes.

Training your Friesian Horse to become the kind of Horse you want him to be while riding him later is a major component of socializing him. The first several months of his training form him into the Friesian Horse he eventually becomes. As a result, you should put in the most effort and concentrate on your final objective during this time. Therefore, ensure you have a strategy, follow it, be consistent, and be clear about what you expect from him. When he follows your instructions, show genuine happiness and excitement by rewarding him generously for his good behavior.

You'll be astounded at your ability to teach your new Friesian horse if you adhere to these principles. Creating the unique link you wish to have with your Friesian Horse for the remainder of his life is another important aspect of socializing. This can only be accomplished by showing him you are the herd's leader. However, you also want to let him know you are best friends and love him. Your Friesian Horse will grow up to be the most devoted and caring companion you have ever had if you follow the proper training methods recommended in this manual and immediately treat him like a best friend. Be sure to demonstrate your dominance as the head of the herd and your want to be friends with this Friesian Horse as you approach social interactions. Maintain your firmness while remaining soft. Give instructions without being harsh or aggressive. When training a Friesian horse, firmness is always preferable to aggression.

How and When to Introduce Your Friesian Horse to Others

Even just a few hours newborn, your Friesian Horse has already started the socialization process. He interacts with his mother and, if any other horses are available, a few horses until then. Naturally, a Friesian horse cannot only expect his mother to teach him how to ride well. From a young age, the Friesian Horse must be exposed to and acclimated to human touch. Mainly because your Friesian Horse's development is greatly influenced by this period of his life, which is also the most impressionable when you welcome your Friesian Horse into your life; he is a little older, so don't stress about how well you trained him. All it will take is a little more time from you. You must begin treating your Friesian horse as the alpha from the moment you acquire him. Talk to him, touch him, and move his body. Get him used to being handled by humans. Each time you remove him from his stall, give him a brush. He'll discover that you're harmless, that this is fun, and that he can trust his new human herdsman. Give your Friesian

Horse a variety of environmental experiences. Take him on rides outside or stroll along a path with lots of grass, plants, animals, and other people strolling, exploring, and having picnics. Take him to your neighborhood lake, the beach, a stream, a pond, etc. Here's the main idea. Play around with it, be imaginative, and show him a variety of environments, including beaches, trails, and natural surroundings. Depending on your situation, he might be exposed to a slow-moving car if you have to go along a gravel road to reach a trail.

The noises your Friesian Horse may be exposed to include traffic, airplanes, trains, and cars. He will grow accustomed to the various settings and noises he encounters. Transporting your Friesian Horse on a horse trailer could be necessary if you are moving him to different locations. This trains him to be intrigued instead of fearful of a wide range of unfamiliar and unusual things. A good horse is a worldwide Friesian.

Allow your Friesian Horse to meet your guests so they can become accustomed to them and learn to enjoy a variety of people. You don't want him to grow unduly dependent on you to the point that he starts to doubt other people. Your Friesian Horse will bring you two closer together if you take the time to bond with it. It also teaches him how to behave with you and others in an appropriate and inappropriate way. It tells him that you are a kind, dependable owner who values him and that spending time with you is joyful and enjoyable. It's a good idea to locate and develop various mentally and physically demanding activities to keep him interested and busy. Note: Spending time alone with your Friesian Horse is essential. This helps him learn that it's OK to be nervous when you're not around to form a bond. Let him graze alone in his paddock or pasture for at least an hour or two a couple of times a day. Please do not approach him, whether by himself or with other horses.

To stop negative behaviors in your Friesian Horse early on:

Don't be scared to correct them.

Tell him "No" forcefully if he nips your arm.

When he fidgets when being touched at the hitching rail, tell him "No."

Early instruction on what is acceptable and unacceptable can help him become a more obedient horse and reduce the need for corrective action in the future.

He will learn that you are in charge and that he must pay attention to you if you stop any negative behavior and start a positive one in its place. Believe it or not, he craves this from you. Start by telling him what actions are appropriate and what are not. Be stern but not mean.

Yelling and harsh punishment should be avoided since these behaviors can cause lifelong stress to your Friesian Horse. You want him to respect you with pride in his heart, not to be terrified of you. To discipline a Friesian horse, all you need to do is give them a strong "No" and redirect them to something else to do. It's now appropriate to begin your Friesian Horse's light training. Naturally, we go into great detail about that in this book on horse training.

Additionally, show him around his stall and paddock and explain that they are secure places for him to go for solitude and weather protection. Never use the paddock as a punishment; otherwise, you risk instilling in him a deep dislike and a lifelong avoidance of it. You will quickly discover that your Friesian Horse adores his paddock and connects it to fresh water, hay, grains, vitamins, and safety.

You will need to plan a farm call from your trusted veterinarian to check that your Friesian Horse is up to date on worming and immunizations and in good health. Pay attention to any advice regarding nutrition, exercise, training, and health issues.

When your Friesian Horse's hooves grow longer, keep an eye out and make an appointment with your reliable farrier to trim them. Pay attention to every piece of advice, such as if your Friesian Horse would benefit from wearing shoes or has strong hooves. Here are some suggestions that you may decide to heed.

You must start seriously training your Friesian Horse when he becomes accustomed to his paddock. That is to say, you can now teach him things on a long lead line or in a circular enclosure with success. We'll go into great detail about this in our next chapters. To help him become acclimated to his surroundings, make sure you stroll with him. To help him overcome his concerns and learn to accept the world as it is, expose him to a wide range of people, horses, and locations. The Friesian Horse socializes throughout its whole life. You can't keep him in the paddock, never let him interact with people, and then expect him to act normally when he does. It takes a lifetime to socialize and teach a Friesian horse. Daily little steps will make a big difference.

Fear Embracing and Getting Over It

Remember that horses experience periods of fear imprinting. In these stages, phobias may emerge in your Horse. Any unfavorable stimuli have the potential to permanently damage your Horse, giving him a lifelong terror.

For example, if a guy mistreats your Friesian Horse at this age, he may develop a fear of all men. If a child is constantly tugging on his tail, he may develop a fear of children.

Try to keep your Friesian Horse from being afraid of anything that scares him, such as loud noises like fireworks on July 4th, shouting in rage, or behaviors that could cause him pain but can be avoided. At no point in his life should you be overly strict with him; instead, be kind. Take him on frequent walks around the stables to expose him to normal environmental stimuli, such as traffic and loud music, to help him overcome his scared attitude and learn that most stimuli are harmless. He will become less fearful as you expose him to the outside world.

Naturally, some horses experience strange phobias. My Horse became fearful when he was left alone in the stables without any other horses to accompany him. Every day, I took him farther and farther. I would force him to go a little farther and stand for five minutes every day before I came back. I kept saying, "Good boy, good boy, good boy," to him each time. After about five minutes, we had moved out enough that he could not see the other horses. We carried on for an hour-long trail ride as he didn't appear to be experiencing any more concerns about it. He never again felt afraid to go out on his own. It took an entire bag of goodies for both of us to get over that one. On the bright side, we did manage to get a good amount of exercise.

For example, as happened to one of my horses, your Friesian Horse may develop anxiety when they walk over a tarp on the grass. I wonder whether he was afraid he would trip, fall, or slip. For whatever reason, he refused to use the tarp as a walkway. This was resolved when he saw that another horse was led over the tarp, and the animal had not suffered any harm. His eyes showed surprise, and his ears sprang straight up. After that, he never again felt afraid of it since he followed the other Horse over the tarp. Always repeatedly tell him, "good boy," whenever he conquers a fear. Let him understand that he won't be harmed by the things he fears. Assist him in forming constructive associations rather than destructive ones.

Your Friesian Horse may develop timidity if he has a negative encounter with a person, Horse, or animal. However, if you take the time to help him overcome this fear and recondition him, it need not last forever.

It's good to show him that not everyone is the Unabomber by exposing him to horses, other animals, and nice, joyful people. For obvious reasons, you should avoid someone who yelled at your Friesian Horse while they were at the stables. Help him get over his phobia of people by exposing him to other calmer, more gentle individuals. A vital component of socializing your Friesian Horse is helping him overcome his fear.

You might also want to show him other aspects of who you are. You can shave it off and wear a hat if you're an adult male with a beard. In addition, if you so choose (I heard it grows back thicker). Instead of pants or jeans, you can wear a dress, shorts, or sunglasses.

You can even switch up your hairstyle, shampoo, and aftershave by using a different scent. He'll be aware of these modifications. He will accept that occasionally, your appearance or aroma changes if you keep talking to him and reassure him that everything is OK when you look different. He won't be as anxious about change after that.

Continue reading to learn how to look after your new best buddy.

Quick Tip: Grooming Horses

When grooming a horse, exercise caution if you use a hair conditioner (like Show Sheen) for more shine. Always be careful not to use excessive amounts. Additionally, avoid putting it on your Horse's girth or back since this might cause the saddle to slip, which could lead to an accident where you fall off your Horse. Taking precautions like this when grooming your Horse helps keep you safe and lessens the stress on the animal in the event of an accident.

Hold On To A Black Horse.

Check out these techniques to maintain your black Horse's deep, dark coat color if you're concerned about it fading as summer approaches.

When the Horse goes outside, cover him with a fly sheet.

Feed Paprika to the Horse.

Do not let the Horse out in the sun for too long.

Make use of shampoo designed specifically for horses with dark coats.

Shiny Tips for Horse Coats

Your Horse should have a gorgeous, lustrous summer coat by now if you have been giving him the right care. The reason it's shiny is that the vigorous brushing has spread the oil from his coat throughout the whole hair length. It can also be because you didn't give him many baths during the winter.

Furthermore, the summer heat hasn't yet reached a strong enough temperature to bleach out hair, leaving it lifeless and brittle.

Use a rubber curry to massage the oil into the coat, a firm brush to remove dust, and a soft brush to remove any remaining dust particles to maintain your Horse's glossy coat. After gathering up the fine dust with a little damp cloth, place the hair down.

Not taking a bath is another important secret to a glossy coat. Similar to what happens to human hair, over-washing your Horse's coat removes all of the oil and leaves it looking dull and dry. Thus, when your Horse is sweaty and muddy after a ride, rinse him off, ideally with cool water, rather than giving him a soap bath. More oil is removed from the water when it is hotter.

Using a hair conditioner instead of oil while bathing him is crucial. It also helps to treat your Horse with hot oil once every three months. Although a product is available for purchase, using baby oil in hot water is equally effective.

After applying it to your Horse and letting it sit for a few days, remove it with a mild shampoo. Do not plan to go to a show when the oil is in his coat because the oil attracts dust. But after the oil is removed, the coat has an extraordinary sheen and brightness.

Let Your Horse Talk

Teaching a horse to open his lips for bridling, deworming, and general health or age assessments is crucial. Many horses, especially the younger ones, will not like having their mouths touched, but they will have to learn to accept it.

First, make sure your Horse is in a safe location. Ensure you have adequate workspace and are not crammed into a small space. To get the Horse acquainted with you stroking his head, start by rubbing his face, muzzle, nose, and ears. It's becoming less painful. You can also toy with his lips and wiggle them while stroking his chin. He becomes accustomed to using his mouth that way.

The more time you spend simply massaging a horse's head, the less likely it is that you will experience head shyness or bridling problems later on. Once a horse is comfortable being handled, tie him up, wrap one arm around his nose, and press the outside of his mouth with the other hand to urge him to open his lips. To avoid those rear molars, keep them close to the outside of his mouth.

Hold onto the Horse's nose even if he throws his head. If you can, put him in a kind of headlock. This is mostly psychological. Your Horse will learn to avoid you if you let him toss his head without opening. You have to force him to comply. Simply keep playing with his chin and upper lips until you get the hang of handling him if he doesn't open.

Brilliant Whites for Equines

The health and general performance of horses greatly depend on equine dentistry. According to Idea Marketers, there are four factors for healthy horse teeth.

Enhance the functionality of the Horse's mouth to ensure that it can masticate food correctly and effectively. This will lower the cost of feeding horses because the animal can absorb the most nutrients from the feed.

To optimize equine performance, enhance the comfort and functionality of the Horse's mouth by ensuring there are no issues that could impede the Horse's ability to move its head anteriorly and posteriorly during movement. Avoiding the potential discomfort that dental issues may cause when riding.

Improving health and welfare by ensuring horses are not in any discomfort or agony. Evolution of the Horse indicates lengthy periods of trickle feeding as the most natural mode of eating; this may be achieved in comfort with a suitable dental regimen.

Extending the life of the mouth. Any issue will only worsen because of the Horse's hypsodont teeth's constant eruption. Maintaining a proper dental schedule will keep these issues from worsening and lengthen the teeth' life.

Additionally, show him around his stall and paddock and explain that they are secure places for him to go for solitude and weather protection. Never use the paddock as a punishment; otherwise, you risk instilling in him a deep dislike and a lifelong avoidance of it. You will quickly discover that your Horse adores his paddock and connects it to fresh water, hay, grains, vitamins, and safety.

To ensure your Horse is healthy and up to date on vaccines and worming, you must arrange for your reliable veterinarian to visit the farm. Pay attention to any advice regarding nutrition, exercise, training, and health issues.

Keep an eye on your horses' hooves, and when they grow too long, make an appointment with your reliable farrier to trim them. Pay attention to all advice, even if it says your Horse would benefit from shoes or has strong hooves. Here are some suggestions that you may decide to heed.

Viewpoint (Yours)

Once your Horse has become comfortable in his paddock, you should start teaching him seriously. That is to say, you can now teach him things on a long lead line or in a circular enclosure with success. We'll go into great detail about this in our next chapters. To help him become acclimated to his surroundings, make sure you stroll with him. To help him overcome his concerns and learn to accept the world as it is, expose him to a wide range of people, horses, and locations. The Horse socializes for the whole of its life. You can't keep him in the paddock, never let him interact with people, and then expect him to act normally when he does. It takes a lifetime to socialize and train your Horse. Daily little steps will make a big difference.

Fear Embracing and Getting Over It

Remember that horses experience periods of fear imprinting. In these stages, phobias may emerge in your Horse. Any unfavorable stimuli have the potential to permanently damage your Horse, giving him a lifelong terror.

For example, if a guy mistreats your Horse during this phase, he may develop a fear of all men. If a child is constantly tugging on his tail, he may develop a fear of children.

Try to keep your Horse from being scared by things that terrify him, such as loud noises like fireworks on July 4th, shouting in rage, or activities that could cause him unnecessary harm. At no point in his life should you be overly strict with him; instead, be kind. Take him on frequent walks around the stables to expose him to normal environmental stimuli, such as traffic and loud music, to help him overcome his scared attitude and learn that most stimuli are harmless. He will become less fearful as you expose him to the outside world.

Naturally, some horses experience strange phobias. My Horse became fearful when he was left alone in the stables without any other horses to accompany him. Every day, I took him farther and farther. I would force him to go a little farther and stand for five minutes every day before I came back. I kept saying, "Good boy, good boy, good boy," to him each time. After about five minutes, we had moved out enough that he could not see the other horses. We carried on for an hour-long trail ride as he didn't appear to be experiencing any more concerns about it. He never again felt afraid to go out on his own. It took an entire bag of goodies for both of us to get over that one. On the bright side, we did manage to get a good amount of exercise.

For example, your Horse may develop anxiety when it crosses a tarp on the lawn. I wonder whether he was afraid he would trip, fall, or slip. For whatever reason, he refused to use the tarp as a walkway. This was resolved when he saw that another horse was led over the tarp, and the animal had not suffered any harm. His eyes showed surprise, and his ears sprang straight up. After that, he never again felt afraid of it since he followed the other Horse over the tarp. Always repeatedly tell him, "good boy," whenever he conquers a fear. Let him understand that he won't be harmed by the things he fears. Assist him in forming constructive associations rather than destructive ones.

Your Horse may develop timidity if he has a negative encounter with a person, another horse, or any other animal. However, if you take the time to help him overcome this fear and recondition him, it need not last forever.

It's good to show him that not everyone is the Unabomber by exposing him to horses, other animals, and nice, joyful people. For obvious reasons, you would want to avoid someone who is frequenting the stables and yelling at your Horse, for instance. Help him get over his phobia of people by exposing him to other calmer, more gentle individuals. The first step in socializing your Horse is to help him overcome his fear.

You might also want to show him other aspects of who you are. You can shave it off and wear a hat if you're an adult male with a beard. In addition, if you so choose (I heard it grows back thicker). Instead of pants or jeans, you can wear a dress, shorts, or sunglasses.

You can even switch up your hairstyle, shampoo, and aftershave by using a different scent. He'll be aware of these modifications. He will accept that occasionally, your appearance or aroma changes if you keep talking to him and reassure him that everything is OK when you look different. He won't be as anxious about change after that.

Continue reading to learn how to look after your new best buddy.

Giving up

Sacking is a popular technique for teaching horses that elicits differing opinions from trainers. Desensitizing the Horse to objects and situations that frighten them is part of the technique. Untrained horses are typically terrified of many things in the contemporary world, such as passing cars, floating paper bags, and loud music. When horses feel threatened by anything, they naturally fight or flee. For cyclists, this poses a serious risk in most situations. In such levels of fear, riders may get injuries from horses.

The purpose of sacking is to acquaint the Horse with these terrifying objects. Thus, in circumstances when they otherwise may become scared, this aids the horses in maintaining their composure. The Horse is taught to be curious about their surroundings and the frightening phenomenon rather than reacting rashly with a fight-or-flight response.

In a standard sacking session, the trainer will provide the Horse with an object it would typically be afraid of, allow it to sniff it, and even massage it. This is to assist the Horse in realizing that the object is safe. After the Horse has become accustomed to the paper bag, the trainer will release it and see how the animal responds. Exposing the Horse to such objects regularly teaches them that there is nothing to fear.

Even while sacking is a valuable tool in horse training, many trainers oppose it because they believe it is cruel.

Work on liberty

The primary belief is that liberty labor is a kind of longing. During liberty work, the Horse learns to always obey the trainer's cues, whether from the ground or while riding. The Horse is exercised in a round pen without a rope for guidance. The activity is known as "liberty work" because it allows the participant to walk around the round enclosure without being tied to anything. Since the trainer aims to gain the Horse's understanding and enable unfettered communication, liberty work is regarded as a natural horsemanship discipline.

Primary Ground Training Goals

The trainer's goal in ground training is to acquaint the Horse with human companionship and touch. It is crucial to remember that you must touch and have close contact with a horse to be able to ride it. Common exercises include:

Caressing the Horse all over.

Giving it scratches.

Introducing and tying it to a saddle to help it become accustomed to it.

The Horse can also be introduced to ropes; it can be flung over or wrapped around its feet. The Horse gets acclimatized to regular care through these workouts.

Comprehending human body language and gestures is another important learning gained from ground training exercises. Using basic motions, the trainer will attempt to get the Horse to halt, move more quickly, slowly, or even turn around. The primary motions used here include, among others, finger-pointing and hand gestures. The trainer will strive to have the Horse follow orders without any contact. Getting the Horse to approach or retreat from the trainer may also entail swinging a rope.

Numerous physical impediments will come into contact with you when riding horses. It's critical to have faith that the Horse can clear or stop and go alongside the obstacles. For example, a horse should be able to side-pass next to a wall or fence without misinterpreting the rider's intentions.

Regular riding also includes navigating tight areas. Ground training aims to teach the Horse to stay calm in situations like this so that the rider won't have to risk their lives. The Horse is conditioned to walk fearlessly and confidently in these areas.

The "behind the girth" leg position

A leg aid that provides support, protection, or regulation is called "passive." The opposite "passive" leg informs the Horse how much sideways movement is necessary in response to the lateral driving leg aid, which requests a forward-sideway movement. If the Horse is in a circle, the outside passive leg forms a border or wall to indicate how far his body should travel out to the Horse. Always use the passive leg aid and the lateral-driving leg aid simultaneously. The passive leg aid should support the active leg's greater pressure. The "passive" leg is typically positioned slightly below the perimeter, and pressure is applied to the Horse's side as needed. The Horse's sensibility and degree of training determine where the legs should be placed precisely and how hard to apply them. Start with a small amount of pressure on the Horse's side and work up to the desired response.

The Fundamentals of Horse Training or Horse Retraining

Introduction

"The horse obeys willingly and without hesitation due to a lively impulsion and the suppleness of his joints, free from the paralyzing effect of resistance." FEI

The foundation of all English equestrian sports is dressage, the French term for horse training. It aims to improve a horse's rideability.

One of your primary goals while training a horse is to establish a partnership with him, as we just covered in the book's introduction, so that you can enjoy riding a trustworthy and cooperative animal. You want him to accept your kind assistance and act upon it without hesitation. A horse must be balanced and flexible to fulfill your demands when you give them. Generally speaking, a horse will only rebel if he cannot comply with your request at that particular time or if he is confused by your assistance. A horse can only be fully trusted and respected if treated with patience and firmness rather than force or bullying.

Our training should not disrupt the natural gaits of horses; rather, it should make them more balanced, easy, economical, fluid, and coordinated. Instead of falling forward, we want the Horse to move forward using his hindquarters. More weight over the hind legs preserves the joints of the forehand from too much hammering. Moreover, it improves a horse's balance and ability to stop, turn, change gaits, and practically do anything else. He rides more comfortably and enjoyably as a result.

Once you've established the desired outcome for your Horse's teaching, the next concern is figuring out how to reach this level of proficiency. If you follow these schooling procedures, your Horse will be physically and mentally ready for anything you ask him to perform (dressage, show jumping, eventing/horse trials, hacking, etc.). The training will get more specialized later on, but as long as the fundamentals are understood, it should be easy to continue and diversify the training to higher levels.

There are phases to the progression of basic training. The time it takes to get to each level varies depending on the particular Horse as well as the regularity and caliber of the training. No matter how naturally gifted a horse may be, his training cannot be advanced if he is only ridden sometimes. Try to work your Horse four or five days a week minimum. A horse does not transition smoothly from one stage to the next at a set time. The phases are worked through gradually; you might be working on two or three levels at once, but be careful that every new exercise or movement you ask the Horse to perform doesn't go far beyond what you have already taught him. If you ask questions of your Horse too soon before he is psychologically or physically prepared to answer them, you risk encountering issues later. Naturally, there are moments when you need to give your Horse a bit more push to advance to the next level. As long as he doesn't get agitated and show you that he's not ready to move on, this is all OK. You should anticipate that your Horse will find certain training exercises easier and others harder. It is improbable that a horse will advance through its training phases trouble-free and without mishaps. Horses advance, get stuck, or even regress sometimes in their training. They might easily get through one or two stages before being stuck. Don't keep your Horse doing the same exercises repeatedly; give him time to figure out the issues and advance to the next level.

When retraining an older horse, work him through the phases from the beginning like a young horse. He will advance swiftly until he reaches the area of his training that, for whatever reason, was skipped over during his first instruction. In this case, the older Horse will probably need to learn the proper method of doing things and give up an established "bad" habit. It may take some time, and frequently, it could seem like things are becoming worse rather than better. The right muscles will be developed via patient and regular practice, enabling him to complete the tasks necessary to advance to the next level.

Flatwork (dressage) and jumping training go hand in hand, but any errors already present "on the flat" will be magnified while jumping. For all English equestrian sports, it is crucial to master the fundamental flatwork because many issues related to jumping stem from improper basic dressage practice.

Starting as a foal, the young Horse must complete some fundamental education before beginning the ride instruction under the saddle. A foal must learn to live in a stable environment, tolerate human contact, groom, wear a headcollar, follow hands, and do other things. Gaining the trust of a young horse can be challenging, and issues are likely to arise if careless or ignorant handlers consistently make mistakes at this early period.

The initial training of a horse begins when it is a foal.

Before the child is ridden, this introduction acclimates him to various tools, including a bridle, saddle, roller, brushing boots, bandages, and more. The Horse is introduced to free-schooling and lungeing in a fenced arena, lunge ring, or round pen. It is not as simple to lunge correctly as it may appear. If done incorrectly, lunging a horse can cause harm and takes great experience.

A young horse can learn acceptance and tranquility through lungeing.

The young Horse is being mounted and ridden for the first time when appropriate. The young Horse must take on the rider's weight and support him primarily with his back, neck, and abdomen muscles. These muscle groups need to be gradually built up over the coming months with appropriate exercises because they are still weak and untrained. The Horse is prepared for the first phase of his rode basic training when he can walk and trot on straight lines and large circles for up to fifteen minutes while carrying the rider comfortably and voluntarily.

Chapter 3: A Brief Introduction to Your Andalusian Horse

How to Train Your Andalusian Horse to Be Socially Comfortable

It is crucial to socialize your Andalusian Horse from a young age. Are you aware of the reason? Because a well-socialized Andalusian horse does not react negatively toward or fear dogs or people. He is aware that both people and dogs exist and do not always threaten his safety. UnsocializedAndalusian horses, on the other hand, perceive the outside world as a threat and respond with terror. The presence of people or other canines frightens and threatens him. Thus, you must begin socializing your Andalusian Horse when you bring him home. Acclimate him to living with pets and other people.

Viewpoint (Yours)

Your Andalusian Horse can tell a lot about your attitude. You are like a book to him. He can tell when you are angry with him. Additionally, he can detect when you are upset and won't accept that it isn't related to him. As a result, you should always be forceful and have a positive attitude while socializing. When your Andalusian Horse senses your positive energy, they bond more closely. Be kind, loving, patient, and supportive at all times.

Express your pride and joy more than your annoyance or dissatisfaction. If you are frustrated, take a moment to move away, breathe deeply, and engage in a different activity with your Andalusian Horse. When you're feeling composed, go back. Your secret to success while training your Andalusian Horse will be positivity. You will damage the training experience and the overall results for both of you if you continue to push your Andalusian Horse or lose your temper.

Conditioning your Andalusian Horse to become the kind of Horse you want him to be while riding him later on is a major component of socializing him. The first few months of training transform him into the Andalusian Horse he eventually becomes. As a result, you should put in the most effort and concentrate on your final objective during this time. Therefore, ensure you have a strategy, follow it, be consistent, and be clear about what you expect from him. When he follows your instructions, show genuine happiness and excitement by rewarding him generously for his good behavior.

If you adhere to these principles, you'll be astounded at your ability to teach your new Andalusian Horse. Developing the unique relationship you wish to have with your Andalusian Horse for the entirety of his life is another important aspect of socializing. This can only be accomplished by showing him you are the herd's leader. However, you also want to let him know you are best friends and love him. Your Andalusian Horse will grow up to be the most devoted and caring buddy you have ever had if you follow the training methods recommended in this manual and immediately treat him like a best friend. When you approach social situations, pretend that you want to be friends with this Andalusian Horse, but don't forget to assert your dominance and leadership over the group. Maintain your firmness while remaining soft. Give instructions without being harsh or aggressive. Aggression is never a better socialization strategy for Andalusian horses than firmness.

When and How to Introduce Your Horse to Others

Even as a few hours old, your Andalusian Horse has already started the socialization process. He interacts with his mother and, if any other horses are available, a few horses until then. Naturally, an Andalusian horse cannot simply expect his mother to teach him to ride well. From a young age, the Andalusian Horse must be introduced to and acclimated to human touch mainly because your Andalusian Horse's development is greatly influenced by this period of his life, which is also the most impressionable. He is a little older when you bring your Andalusian Horse into your life. Don't stress about how well you trained him. All it will take is a little more time from you. When you acquire him, you must treat your Andalusian Horse correctly as the alpha. Talk to him, touch him, and move his body. Get him used to being handled by humans. Each time you remove him from his stall, give him a brush. He'll discover that you're harmless, that this is fun, and that he can trust his new human herdsman. Give your Andalusian Horse a variety of environmental experiences. Take him on rides outside or stroll along a path with lots of grass, plants, animals, and other people strolling, exploring, and having picnics. Take him to your neighborhood lake, the beach, a stream, a pond, etc. Here's the main idea. Play around with it, be imaginative, and show him a variety of environments, including beaches, trails, and natural surroundings. Depending on your situation, he might be exposed to a slow-moving car if you have to go along a gravel road to reach a trail.

Your Andalusian Horse may hear sounds from vehicles, trains, planes, and traffic. He will grow accustomed to the various settings and noises he encounters. Transporting your Andalusian Horse on a horse trailer can be necessary if you plan to take him to other environments. This teaches him that being curious is OK instead of being scared of a wide range of unfamiliar and unusual things. An excellent horse is an Andalusian with a worldly outlook.

Allow your Andalusian Horse to get to know your guests so he can develop tolerance for various personalities. You don't want him to grow unduly dependent on you to the point that he starts to doubt other people. Your Andalusian Horse will firmly bind the two of you together, so take the time to develop your relationship with it. It also teaches him how to behave with you and others in an appropriate and inappropriate way. It tells him that you are a kind, dependable owner who values him and that spending time with you is joyful and enjoyable. It's a good idea to locate and develop various mentally and physically demanding activities to keep him interested and busy. It's important to spend some alone time with your Andalusian Horse. This helps him learn that it's OK to be nervous when you're not around to form a bond. Let him graze alone in his paddock or pasture for at least an hour or a couple of times a day or two. Please do not approach him, whether by himself or with other horses.

To avoid undesirable habits in your Andalusian Horse early on:

Don't be hesitant to correct them.

Tell him "No" forcefully if he nips your arm.

When he fidgets when being touched at the hitching rail, tell him "No."

Early instruction on what is acceptable and unacceptable can help him become a more obedient horse and reduce the need for corrective action in the future.

He will learn that you are in charge and that he must pay attention to you if you stop any negative behavior and start a positive one in its place. Believe it or not, he craves this from you. Start by telling him what actions are appropriate and what are not. Be stern but not mean.

Steer clear of shouting and physical punishment; these behaviors might permanently traumatize your Andalusian Horse. You want him to respect you with pride in his heart, not to be terrified of you. When disciplining your Andalusian Horse, all it takes is a strong "No" and a redirection to another activity to correct a behavior. It's now appropriate to begin your Andalusian Horse's light training. Naturally, we go into great detail about that in this book on horse training.

Additionally, show him around his stall and paddock and explain that they are secure places for him to go for solitude and weather protection. Never use the paddock as a punishment; otherwise, you risk instilling in him a deep dislike and a lifelong avoidance of it. You will quickly discover that your Andalusian Horse adores his paddock and connects it to fresh water, hay, grains, vitamins, and safety.

To ensure your Andalusian Horse is in good health and has received all its vaccines and wormings, you must arrange for your reliable veterinarian to visit the farm. Pay attention to any advice regarding nutrition, exercise, training, and health issues.

When your Andalusian Horse's hooves begin to get longer, keep an eye out and make an appointment with your reliable farrier for a hoof trim. Pay attention to all advice, even if it says your Andalusian Horse would benefit from shoes or has powerful hooves. Here are some suggestions that you may decide to heed.

Tips for Beginning Equine Trainers

Horse training aims to gradually get your horse's attention and teach him the skills you want from him. You want the horse to regard you as its lead mare, regardless of the owner's or the animal's gender. Training your horse can be difficult if he is a born leader. Naturally, a horse requires a leader to advise them on what to do and how things should be. All of that comes with being a social animal. It should be obvious that you are in charge of this situation. The horse will regard you as a leader out of fear or deference. But as a leader, you want to gain your horse's respect via connections and interaction.

It often receives no official training until a horse is two years old. However, foals can learn how to behave around people at an early age. Your horse will become accustomed to being around you and eventually start interacting with people if you spend as much time as possible with him.

You commence with the fundamentals when your equine becomes old enough to begin training. You don't try to ride him. It's not yet time to mount the horse. The initial step in the training procedure is lengthening, or ground training, using long ropes. As you teach the horse orders, he can move in a wide circle thanks to the longer wire that fastens to his reins.

Teaching your horse to follow you by the side is another crucial lesson. Teaching a horse to turn and stop at your command is known as lead training. You will use this daily with your horse, and it is essential. During lead training, some horses will put you to the test by attempting to push you out of their space. Never let him get away with it. The further training that comes later will be challenging if he rejects this simple instruction.

Ridden horses must be trained to follow their rider's cues. Your horse must comply with requests for it to do things. This will eliminate the need for a crop or whip to correct or motivate the horse. You don't have to worry about training sessions being too lengthy or too short because there are no defined times for them. But remember, horses also require rest.

The first part of training should be spent getting the horse mentally and physically warmed up. This horse requires time to warm up its muscles and loosen its joints. Cravings are frequently employed to acclimate a horse.

Everything the horse has learned from the earlier training sessions should be covered in the second half of the session. Adding new skills to the horse's repertoire as slight modifications are possible. Making progress on previously acquired abilities is essential to training your horse effectively.

You want the horse to see new equipment, like a saddle, but you have to remove it after a short while. This will need to be done again for a few days. You want the horse to stay fearless and acclimate to the new equipment. Then, let the horse put it on as it heats up. After he gets the hang of putting on the saddle, have someone sit on him while he's motionless for a little while. With the rider back up, complete the sprint. Incorporate something fresh, but just for a brief while.

A drill is another item of equipment you'll need to progressively add. It takes time for horses to grow acclimated to something in their mouths, like a saddle. Equine mouths must acclimate to swallowing saliva while holding strange things in their mouths. For everything to go smoothly, the trainer will gradually introduce the mouthpiece, limiting its use to a few minutes first, then gradually increasing it until the horse stops rejecting it.

Another item of gear that needs to be acclimated to gradually is the saddle. You will first remove the stirrups and leather. Put the saddle on the horse after demonstrating it to him. Hold off on touching him with the saddle until he stops being fearful. When you first put a saddle on a horse, be ready for a lot of pats and caressing. The girth, leather, and stirrups must be added the next time the saddle is mounted on the horse. You should introduce new saddles only after the horse has overcome his fear of the previous one. It will take some time, so try not to get frustrated.

After every training session, there should be a cooling-off period. When the training is going well, and the horse starts to feel weary and irritated, that is when you want the cooling-off break to start. The horse will have time to relax and recoup during the cooling-off phase, both physically and emotionally. You want the training session to remain enjoyable in your horse's memory. End the training session in a way that will make the horse remember all the good things about it. Now would be a good time to let the horse play before putting him back in the stable or pasture.

Remember that the horse will pick up cues from you, so maintain your composure and bravery. Also, your horse will feel fearless and at ease. If you move, the horse will follow you, sensing that you are the lead mare changing directions. The horse will follow you instinctively once it catches your body language. There are guidelines in horse training that tell you how to use and discipline your horse. Training horses is both an art and a science.

Once your horse has been trained to comply with your commands, you should avoid giving him the same instruction too frequently. That order and subsequent behavior would irritate the horse, making him reluctant to repeat it. Ask him to complete the task a couple more times after he completes it, but don't give up and stop asking. Not too many times a day, though. You can give the same order and ask him to perform the same deed again. After that, you assign him another task. You want him to enjoy himself during the training. You don't want to train your horse to become disinterested or difficult to work with.

Before working with your horse, you must also evaluate his character. Understanding what a pupil is like before you begin teaching him is important.

Rewarding the horse right away is necessary if it appears anxious. Petting him frequently is important if you want to keep him confident. Be careful when utilizing assistive aids.

If your horse has a mischievous disposition, you must be patient and persistent in getting him to comply with your requests.

You can see how crucial it is to be aware of your horse's condition before beginning any training. You'll operate more effectively.

It is your responsibility as a horse trainer to make every effort to assist your horse in learning the tasks you ask of him. You must get to know your horse and choose the best way to support his learning to accomplish this.

6. Recognizing Horse Breeds and Their Purposes

When purchasing a horse, you should examine the purpose you want to utilize him and the role his breed intended. When examining horses, there are a few things to take into account. Among them are:

Conformation (the skeletal system's anatomy as a result of his breeding)

Kindness or indifference in personality, possibly due to handling or breeding

Training—to what extent has he received training?

Nature: passive or active? Subservient or dominating?

Breeding (bloodlines) and/or environment (training/handling or lack thereof) might contribute to these fundamental traits.

Even if each horse is unique in appearance and temperament, you can make better selections if you know his lineage and, consequently, his intended purpose.

For instance, you should remember that thoroughbreds are mostly the product of centuries of breeding for a quick racehorse if you're considering purchasing one. This implies that the thoroughbred might exhibit high reactivity, responsiveness, and sensitivity levels. This is not to suggest that quiet thoroughbreds aren't out there. Those horses typically did not fare well on the track and could produce excellent sports horses. They are frequently built to fit easily into hunting, eventing, dressage, and other disciplines due to their breeding. Several thoroughbreds have also delighted in their peaceful walks along the pathways. But it turns out that most thoroughbreds have exactly what their breeding intended: a highly sensitive, tense temperament and a ready demeanor. However, a racehorse can also have several advantages, like a history of regular daily treatment, including being led, saddled, halter broken, bathed, and handled by a farrier.

Another example of breed affecting intended use may be the draft horse, hackney, or morgan bred to pull a carriage. Rather than carrying riders or jumping, these horses frequently have a conformation designed to aid in pulling. To start the carriage, they might shift their weight onto their shoulders. Such horses may not have a conformation that readily allows them to rock their weight onto their hindquarters to lift their shoulders to take the canter or jump a fence. Numerous historical pulling breeds, such as the Friesian, are built like carriage horses or have been crossed to resemble riding horses. Thus, you must be aware of the riding type's appearance.

The fashion for dressage, jumps, and even hunters has shifted to warmbloods. These European horses are the offspring of centuries-long intermarriage between lighter riding horses and larger carriage horses, producing an athletic, powerful sport horse. The Hanoverian, Swedish, Dutch, and Trakehner are some breeds considered warmbloods. The term "warmblood" originated from the cross between the "cold blood" draft horse and the "hot blood" light-riding horse. The terms refer to the personality traits of the horses, which lean toward being "cold-blooded" (quiet, docile) or "hot-blooded" (reactive, sensitive) rather than anything to do with blood.

What about crosses, then? Fascinating hybrids are becoming more and more common. There is indeed a thoroughbred that competes competitively in eventing and is named Clydesdale. Draft crosses with light breeds are becoming popular. To mention a couple, there are Belgian/quarter horses and Percheron/thoroughbreds. Draft horses were developed to be calm, massive animals that collaborated well with people on farms, hauling carriages and plows, among other odd chores. Because of their size, the horses needed to be bred to be agreeable mates. Therefore, these crossbreeds aim to combine the lighter riding horse's athleticism with the sturdy bone and submissive, willing mind of the draft horse. With careful, intelligent breeding, the crosses can be excellent and conformationally correct mates. As with any other badly bred animal, the result of the cross can be disastrous due to poor breeding. As a result of their recent crosses rather than centuries of breeding to produce a particular type, these breed hybrids are frequently referred to as the American warmblood. (Consider, for example, a high-strung thoroughbred mind in the body of an 18-hand half draft.)

Therefore, if you are considering purchasing a horse, you can use his breeding to help guide your selection. Examine the breed's intended usage and see if it aligns with your intended use, and make sure he is sound and conformationally correct. Not only may this help you make better purchasing decisions, but it might also help you understand why he behaves and is built in a particular way, which could lead to productive working relationships between you both.

Feeding Inventory

✔ Find out the former owner's preferred feed.

✏ Purchase plenty of hay and feed.

✔ Make fresh water available.

✔ Fill a familiar basin with fresh water for the horse.

Moving the Horse

You've built up your stable, acquired the necessary supplies, vaccinated your horse, and bought some food. It's time to return the horse to its home. You have two options for transporting your horse: land or air, depending on how far your horse is from your house. Regardless of the mode of transportation you use, attempt to travel the least distance to reduce the effort of the trip. Using a horse trailer is the most efficient way to move your horse over land. If you don't have one, you can always rent one. Your horse will experience less stress during the move if you use a competent horse moving firm.

Ensure the trailer is comfy for your horse and in good shape before the travel day. The trailer's floor should be non-slip and large enough for your horse to put its head down. If the ride is long, stop periodically so the horse can eat and relax. Use a lead rope or halter to tie the horse securely and to help you load it. Ensure the tie is not too tight to prevent discomfort for the horse. Since horses fear small places, transporting them in a car can be stressful. To prevent this, teach your horse to get in and out of the trailer before the travel day.

Checklist for Transportation

✔ Find the most effective way to return the horse home.

✔ Select a reputable horse relocation company.

✎ Examine the conveyance vehicle.

✔ Make the shortest path possible when planning the trip.

✔ Make sure the horse has enough food and water.

✔ Get your horse some travel boots.

✔ Before moving day, teach the horse how to get in and out of the trailer.

Acclimating the Horse to its New Residence

You and your horse have finally arrived at your destination—your home—after a protracted (or perhaps brief) journey. Your horse must spend the first few days and weeks of its new home settling in and getting to know you. These are crucial actions that will aid with your horse's adjustment to its new residence.

Step 1: Your horse will probably be apprehensive and reluctant to leave the trailer, so this can be difficult. It is preferable to have an experienced person nearby to help and advise you, particularly if this is your first time riding a horse.

Step 2: Walk your horse to the barn gently and patiently and remove his traveling boots. Provide clean water and hay in his stall. Place your new horse so he can view your other horses if you have any other horses.

Consider walking your new horse around the fence if you want to put him in a padlocked pasture so he becomes used to the edge and knows where to get water and feed.

Step 3: Wear boots to safeguard your horse when you wish to turn him out for the first time so he doesn't damage himself or get hurt by other horses. Your horse should face other horses in a locked stall or pasture. That way, he'll be able to talk to the other horses.

For the first several days, leave your new horse in his stall. He'll feel more at ease and secure as a result. Make sure he's getting enough food and water. He's not exercising, so you can reduce his meals to prevent colic.

Step 4: You can get to know him better by grooming him while he's in his stall. You can walk your new horse around the grounds after a few days of ownership. Use a rope and harness to lead him. Watch him closely and let him explore his new surroundings.

It is best not to introduce your new horse to the entire herd at once if you already own more than two horses. Instead, introduce each to them individually as the weeks pass. Although he should be kept apart, horses are gregarious animals that require company.

Step 5: You can think about letting your new horse go with the entire herd if you're positive he has spent much time with you and is more accustomed to the surroundings and other horses. Ensure adequate pasture for every horse to graze comfortably before proceeding. The last thing you want is for the horses to fight over grass and space in a limited pasture. One acre of pasture land is often recommended for each horse.

Step 6: You will need to stay close by and keep a close eye on things to ensure there are no fights or injuries when you let your new horse out with the entire herd. The introductions don't need to be rushed. Look for indications that your new horse is stressed or that the older horses are mistreating him.

Groom the new horse and spend some time getting to know his preferences.

Step 7: For any horse owner, riding their new mount for the first time is usually an exhilarating experience. Your horse should already be at ease with you and the surroundings before you begin to ride. Be slow and gentle with the horse; do not push.

You should continue to get to know your horse, and he should return the favor. Try to keep things as simple as possible for the first few rides by riding a small distance. In time, you will both get used to one another.

STEP 8: Owning a horse gives an outlet to make new acquaintances — fellow horse owners! ObtainMeet other horse owners, share tales and obtain advice and insights on how best to care for your horse. To keep your horse safe, learn from the experience of seasoned riders in training.

Step 9: Most crucial, contact your horse's prior owner or vendor. Let the person know the improvements the horse is making and ask inquiries when unclear about particular behavioral qualities.

Keep a watchful eye on your horse's health and consult a veterinarian when necessary.

www.ingramcontent.com/pod-product-compliance
Lightning Source LLC
Chambersburg PA
CBHW052143110526
44591CB00012B/1844